Single Moms
With TEENAGERS

Vol. 1

This book teaches Single Moms how to raise teenagers to become happy, healthy, and responsible adults. Learn to navigate the land mines and help them to stay on track.

DONNA JOYCE

All Rights Reserved. No part of this publication may be reproduced in any form or by any means, including scanning, photocopying, or otherwise without prior written permission of the copyright holder.
Donna Joyce Spillman
Copyright © 2018

Table of Contents

Introduction – 4

Chapter One – You Are Not Alone Single Mom – 6

Chapter Two – My Teen Hates Me – What Do I Do Now? – 13

Chapter Three – My Teen Is Rebelling – HELP! – 21

Chapter Four – Why Do Things Feel Different Now? – 29

Chapter Five – My Teen's Dad Isn't Around – 39

Chapter Six – How Do I Foster a Good Relationship with My Teen? – 50

Chapter Seven – I'm Worried About My Teen's Friends – 56

Chapter Eight – My Teen Is Not Responsible – 67

Chapter Nine – My Teen Is Not Doing Well in School – 76

Chapter Ten – Encouragement for Single Mothers – 83

Conclusion

Introduction

Dear single mom, I know right now you may be feeling stressed and overwhelmed. Let's face it, raising teenagers is no walk in the park, especially when you are doing it alone.

Before we set out on our journey together, I want to remind you that what your teen is going through is just a phase. I know, I know, it sounds cliché and does not help you feel any better at this point. I can promise you, things will get better, and you will both survive this period in your lives.

Although being a single mom is a real joy and heartache all rolled up together, the good outweighs the bad, and we all take it a day at a time, learning as we go and sometimes hanging by a thread.

This book was written to help you understand you are not alone. There are many of us out here, feeling isolated and lonely as we grapple to raise our kids to be emotionally, mentally, and physically happy – all while doing it ALONE!

If you are struggling with day to day survival while raising your teen as a single mom, I invite you to read this condensed book that is packed with information to help you overcome the obstacles, find the joy, and even laugh at life again.

Take the time to read this book, and you will find yourself empowered with the information you need to make clear, concise steps towards creating a healthier relationship between you and your child.

I will never patronize you and tell you it will be easy. I won't sugarcoat the text, and I promise to stay practical. This book is all about a conversation between you and me – from one single mom to another.

Chapter One
You Are Not Alone Single Mom

You might think you are all alone in your struggles as a single mom, but I am here to tell you, you are not. Right now, there are approximately 13.6 million one-parent family homes in the US. That number represents a lot of parents feeling like they have lost themselves in the sea of parenthood that covers us all.

Although the vast majority of these solo parents are women, men make up around 16% of all single parents living in the United States.

It doesn't matter if you chose to be a single parent or that choice was made for you, it is tough being the sole caregiver of a child, especially when they reach those fun ages when they know just enough to be independent but not near enough to make it on their own.

~Single moms often feel alone~

Ask any single mom of teens what emotion she often feels, and she will likely admit it's loneliness. There is just something about being a single mom that puts us in the corner, strips us of our identity, and makes us feel as if we are the only ones dealing with struggles.

I can't be the only mom who felt intense loneliness each night her child went to sleep, and there was no one there to spend time with in conversation. If you are feeling the same way, then this chapter is going to give you hope and help you cope. Yes, that rhyme was intentional to make you smile!

~Create a network of help~

Whether you are new to being a single mother or have had years of experience, having a support network of help is vital to your very existence. Now is the time to accept those offers of help from family members and friends.

You are going to need someone you can rely on for help, even if that person is only a listening ear. Some women become so determined to do it all on their own; they forget they don't have to be that strong.

Spending time with other single moms or even other adults in general will help
you to overcome those feelings of isolation and make you feel human again.

For years, you have likely been busy doing everything for your child, but now that they are growing older and more independent, you have more time on your hands, which means more time to worry and become depressed.

Many single moms find it helpful to join support groups in their area. Being a member of one of these groups allowed me to understand I was not alone in the struggles and emotions I always seemed to be dealing with while raising my son by myself. Just talking about my issues with others who understood what I was going through made it easier to breathe.

Do not be afraid to reach out to others when you feel lonely or overwhelmed. Those who care for you will be happy to be there for you during those times when you feel like giving up or just need a moment to relax and feel like something other than *just* a mom.

~Preparing for those lonely moments of weakness as a single mom~

For some reason, single moms are often portrayed as desperate women who are pining away for the attention of a man. In reality, many of us do not feel that way at all. After suffering the breakdown of a relationship, many women are not too keen on jumping right back into one.

Although I prided myself on being a strong woman that didn't need a man, there were lonely nights when I longed for the comfort of a strong pair of arms. Times like these are when the loneliness would sink in deeply, and I would feel overwhelmingly alone.

Because many single moms make the conscious decision to avoid serious relationships until their children are grown, dating is often avoided. So, what can you do when those old feelings of longing rear their ugly heads, making you feel desperately in need of attention from the opposite sex?

The key to overcoming these feelings is to stay busy. You may have just spit out your coffee with a large snork of laughter because you believe you are always busy. You may be endlessly working but are you *busy* in a fulfilling way?

I might stay "busy" working my job or cleaning my house, but this does not mean my mind is fully engaged. My busy work, so to speak, may just be a means of filling up my time without getting me anywhere.

~Find what keeps your mind engaged while being a single mom~

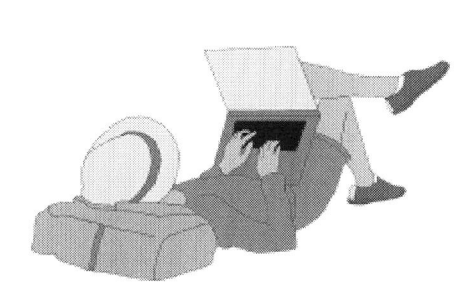

It is essential to find that thing that will keep you busy and keep your mind engaged. There are going to be times when your teen is off doing their own thing, and you need to have a life outside of being a single mom.

Staying busy will also help prepare you for the time your little bird leaves the nest. (I know, we don't want to talk about that just yet.)

First and foremost, you MUST not think of yourself as being selfish because you need a little "me" time. Getting away from parenting for just a little bit does not mean you are selfish, disloyal, or irresponsible.

My mom always told me, you cannot pour from an empty cup. I didn't fully understand this until I became a single mom and began finding myself overwhelmed because I always, always, always put myself last. If you are never taking care of yourself and your own needs, how can you possibly take care of your teen?

As single moms, we tend to sacrifice too much of ourselves to keep our kids happy. While you might believe this to be a noble thing, it ends up leaving you overly tired, overly annoyed and stretched way too thin. Being too tired does not make for happy mothering!

Try finding at least one thing you love doing that will help to occupy your time. It might be a hobby you take up or physical activity, such as running. Even if you only go and watch a single movie with a friend or even alone, you will find this helps you immensely.

As much time and effort as you put into raising your teen, you need to try to put some back for yourself. It is a hard lesson to learn for we single moms who pride ourselves on giving our all to our children. What happens, when everything you have is expended? What will you do then?

Take time for YOU, and you will find you are better able to care for your teen without biting their head off!

Chapter Two
My Teen Hates Me – What Do I Do Now?

I can still recall the first time I heard those words as they were firing from my son's mouth:

"**I HATE YOU!**"

He spit out the words like arrows into my heart and then proceeded to run into his room and slam the door. I couldn't believe he had just said such a thing to me! My child who I:

> Carried for nine months!
> Fed and nurtured!
> Sacrificed for!
> LOVE!

If you have not yet heard these "lovely" words coming from your teen's mouth, you likely will at some point. For some reason, this phrase seems to be a right of passage for teens who suddenly feel they are too old to be told what to do.

After my son hurled those hateful words at me, I can still remember walking calmly into the bathroom, sinking slowly to the floor, and crying my eyes out in panicked, heaving sobs.

What had I done to fail him? Had I not loved him enough? Given him enough? Spent enough time with him? Was I the worst mom on the planet?

My mind started racing over the last fifteen years, attempting to spot my errors as a single mom and pinpoint that defining moment when I had failed so significantly as a single parent that I had caused my son to hate me.

You know what I discovered? Looking back on our relationship between parent and child, I had made many mistakes. I could write an entire book on those mistakes and still have topics to discuss!

I am no perfect mom, and that award will never likely hang in my office or even on my fridge. Being a single mother is tough! Being a mother is hard enough when you have a partner, but it is even more difficult when you are doing everything alone.

The questions that would run through my head each night as I exhaustedly plopped my head on my pillow ran the gamut. Am I making the right choices? Am I too tough on him? Am I tough enough? Am I a good mom? Does he blame me for his dad? Have I messed him up for life?

If these questions have not run through your mind, then you honestly have it much more together than I ever did. Although I would like to think I got "it" together over the years, the truth is, I still question myself even though my son is well past those awkward "terror years" as I call them.

If you get nothing else from this book, I want to let you know…Your teen does not hate you! No matter how much they scream it, no matter how much they yell or stomp their feet, they do not hate you!

~Do not take it personally~

You are likely going to be just like me and immediately begin thinking you are a horrible parent when the child you love so much throws those hateful words at you.

It is essential you realize your teen is only angry. Your child threw those words out to hurt you, and boy did they ever! Once he or she calms down, they will likely feel incredible sadness and regret over those words.

~Do not hurt them back~

As a defense mechanism, we as single moms often find ourselves attempting to ward off criticism because we receive it so much of our lives, from just about everyone. No matter how badly you want to hurl an insult of your own back at your teen, DO NOT do it!

Once those fateful words come spewing from your mouth, you can never take them back! I've talked with many a lone parent who, in anger, has yelled back, "I wish I never had you!"

Believe me, when I say this, you never want to say those words because they will haunt you and your child for the rest of your lives.

Instead of yelling, insulting, or punishing, do whatever you have to do to remain calm. You might need to go into your room, lock the door, and cry into your pillow.

If you are not a crier, it might mean you need to punch your pillow a few times. Getting calm is critical before you take any further steps in dealing with why your teen said what they did to you. The calming process might take hours, or it may even take days. Until you can talk about it without getting angry, do not discuss it with your teen.

~Focus on the reason~

After you have calmed down, this is the perfect time to evaluate your teen's burst of anger. If you argued because of the car or a party invite, then you likely already know the culprit.

It could be the anger is not directed at you at all. Think about what might be going on with school or your teen's personal relationships. Try not to take it personally until you can calmly talk things out.

Your kiddo needs to know in no uncertain terms, saying, "I hate you" is never acceptable. That being said, you do not want to pound home the guilt too much, especially if your teen is already going through emotional turmoil.

Let your teen know how it hurts you to hear those words. Tell them how much you love them and that there are other acceptable ways of showing anger without causing so much pain.

Get to the bottom of it, mom! You are a detective at heart. Asking open-ended questions encourages your teen to talk about why they said what they did.

Teens are not the only age group that tends to say those fateful words. Kids of all ages will. If your teen has hurt you with those words, I challenge you to write down what was said, how it made you feel, and then wad it up and burn it in the fireplace or outside.

~Let it go~

You might think I'm a bit silly, and perhaps you are right, but what I am about to tell you has helped me in dealing with so many negative emotions, including those having to do with my son's father. That is another subject entirely. Yes, I deal with one of "them" too, and it's not usually pretty!

That symbolic act of letting go of the hurt and anger does wonders for the soul. You may never entirely forget the moment, and most likely shouldn't, but there is something to be said of burning it up, so it no longer torments you.

There is also another thing I have done many times over the years in my one parent family. I write letters and never send them.

There is something cathartic about writing a letter to someone and fully expressing how hurt or even enraged you are. Writing a letter gets all of that ugly emotion out and the person the letter was written to never sees it.

You can write the letter on your computer and then delete it, or you can do it the old school way and hand write the message and then burn the paper. Whichever way you choose, I guarantee it will work.

Now, get up off that floor and stop thinking you are a horrible mom! You are amazing, and your child loves you more than you will ever know! One day they will thank you. It might not be now or even in a few years, but one day that thank you will come through, and you will be able to look back on these rough years with rose-colored glasses and a big smile on your face!

Chapter Three
My Teen Is Rebelling – HELP!

If your worst nightmare has come true and your teen has suddenly become rebellious, you likely feel like throwing your hands in the air and giving up. Just about every parent on the planet worries their teen will become rebellious, but I think that fear is even more pronounced in a single family.

Being a single mom is one of the toughest jobs on the planet, and anyone who says otherwise is a fool. If the teen you once loved has slowly evolved into a monster, this chapter is here to help you.

Whether you saw it coming or were blindsided by your kid's rebellion, I want to help you make sense of things while helping you to keep *your* mind and not go insane.

No single mom wants to discover her teen is involved in dangerous behaviors. We tend to blame ourselves when our kids start acting out because we think we must have done something to cause it or we somehow missed the warning signs.

The truth is, teens are sneaky creatures. They are good at hiding things, but a worried mom is better than the FBI at investigating what is going on with her child! God placed that ability within you, so if you suspect something is changing with your kid, keep digging until you learn what is going on.

I had a friend who was a single mom just like me. She was raising a teen daughter, and about the time her daughter was sixteen, things began to change. My friend would call me late at night, sobbing incoherently about what her daughter was putting her through.

Her daughter was drinking, staying out late, and even having sex. My friend felt helpless, but she finally developed a backbone and took control of her home and her life and you can too!

It is a mother's worst nightmare to find her child doing drugs, stealing, or being promiscuous. My friend said she never felt more alone than those nights she spent waiting up for her daughter, worried she would get a call from the police.

~Don't give up single mom~

Right now, you may feel like your life is spiraling out of control. You have discovered your teen is involved in things you could never imagine them doing and now you wonder what you can do to change things.

Some single parents throw up their hands and entirely give up. Although this is the most comfortable route to take, it is certainly not the right thing to do. Think about all the kids in the world who have gone astray merely because they had no parents to care. You are here! You love your child! It's time to fight for them and hold on tighter than you ever thought you would have to hold them!

~Do you need professional help~

Teen rebellion is a truly tough area to offer advice on because each teen and situation is different. First of all, you need to evaluate the severity of the rebellious behavior. Ask yourself these questions:

- Is your teen violent?
- Is your teen engaging in illegal activity?
- Is your teen harming themselves or others?

If you answered yes to any of the above, you need to seek outside professional help and guidance. These behaviors are not something you are going to be able to handle all on your own.

A teen that is threatening self-harm needs a mental health evaluation. There are many ways teens will commit self-harming acts, such as:

- Cutting
- Bulimia
- Anorexia

If you feel your teen is in danger of any kind, do not hesitate in getting professional help. Your teen's life may depend on you getting them professional help before they delve too deep into those dangerous behaviors.

~Should you call the police on your teen~

I can't imagine being in the position of having to call the police on my son, but I would do it in a heartbeat if he were doing something illegal or dangerous. Do not be afraid to get the police involved if your teen becomes violent or destructive in your home. You have a right to protect yourself, and this is the best line of defense against a teen who has lost total control. DO NOT HESITATE!

~What can you do to help~

Okay, so maybe your teen has not yet reached the level of corruption we have been discussing but they are sliding down the slope of rebellion, and you need to know what to do to help them before they slip too far out of your reach.

Giving up is not an option so let's discuss what you can do. Let's go through a list of steps you can begin to take right now so you can regain control of your home and stop allowing your teen to run the show.

- Setting up rules and boundaries is critical for a child of any age, but especially when they reach the teen years. When you are both calm, you need to sit down and agree to a set of rules and the consequences that will come when those rules are broken.

- Give your teen their space. There is nothing worse than barging in on a teen who is angry at you. This action just further fuels the rage and leads to arguments that can be avoided. If your teen is acting out in anger, give them some time in their room to be alone. It is surprising what a little space can do for someone who is in turmoil.

- Getting your teen involved in physical activity is a great way to help them stay centered and to allow for a release of their pent-up anger. Encourage them to participate in sports or get them a gym membership.

- Remaining calm when you confront your teen or talk to them about their behavior is vital. If you are both angry and out of control, nothing good will come of the conversation.

- Try to listen to your teen without judging them. In a one-parent family, listening is so crucial for fostering a sound parent and child relationship because the child needs to know they have someone who is on their side. If you are not listening to your teen, you will likely find they do not listen to you.

- Be prepared to be rejected by your teen. Your attempts, no matter how heartfelt, might fall on deaf ears. If they do, do not take it personally. Remember, teenage angst will only last temporarily, and it will eventually begin to die off. Yes, I promise you, it will!

- Even though they might turn you down, make sure your teen knows you are there for them. Invite them for a chat over coffee or a walk in the park to talk. Just knowing you are there for them can make a big difference, even if you do not see it right now.

You do not have to go through this alone. Seek help from a pastor, a counselor, or a friend. Talk with your teen's coach or their teachers. Many single mothers are embarrassed to talk to others because they do not want to be viewed as a failure. You must overcome this mindset!

Just remember, this will not last forever. No matter how insane your teen might be acting right now, no matter how crazy they are making you feel, I promise you it will get better with time.

Even teens who genuinely become entirely rebellious can end up becoming well-rounded, healthy adults. Every teen goes through some level of rebellious behavior so do not let this undermine you as a single parent. You are still in control!

Never give up and never stop pushing your teen to be all they can be! In a few years, you and your teen will be able to sit down and maybe even laugh a bit about all you went through on this journey.

One day, your child may just have a child of their own, and they will likely recall this period in their life and realize what they put you through. Hopefully, they will learn useful parenting skills from you so they will be able to make it through just like you will!

Chapter Four
Why Do Things Feel Different Now?

It almost seems like it happens overnight. One minute your kid adores you and the next minute, it looks like they can't stand you. When adolescence begins, kids often announce its arrival with dramatic changes to their behavior.

Suddenly, the relationship between parent and child feels strained. I can entirely remember looking at my son one day as I tried interacting with him and realized something had changed.

The boy that used to smile and light up when he saw me now barely gave me a passing glance and I could not understand why. When I would attempt to talk to him or ask him questions, I often received grumbled replies, if anything at all.

He would sometimes scream at me for no reason, and almost everything I did or said seemed to make him angry. At one point, I felt like my being around him at all made him worse.

I must admit, I was in no way prepared for this. I had survived diaper changes, teething, stomach viruses, and the terrible twos, but I was floored when my son suddenly became a stranger to me.

I want you to know I did not handle things as well as I would like to say I did. I took it personally when I shouldn't have. Once again, I found myself questioning my ability to be a single mother.

I finally had to come to realize it wasn't me...it was him. His body was going through massive changes, and he didn't know how to handle it, and neither did I. Looking back, I should have been a little more understanding.

~Think back to your own adolescence~

Making the change over to adolescence is not an easy feat. If you can remember back to your journey, you might be able to see some of the same behaviors you had, in your teen.

I cringe every time I think about my transition. It was not a long one, but it was undoubtedly rememberable.

For about six months, I was always angry at my mother, no matter what she did.

I would just look at her and get angry. I would wonder to myself why I was acting in such a way and I could not make sense of it. I am sure my mother couldn't either.

My mom always said it was the roughest period of my growing up. She was a solo parent and trying to raise two kids without any help from my dad. She worked two jobs to make ends meet and here I was giving her hell.

Now that she is gone, I often regret those six months. I mainly know how it feels after going through my son's rough period. If only I could turn back time and make things different; sadly, I cannot.

If you went through a tough period when transitioning to adolescence, perhaps this will help you better understand what your kid is going through right now. If nothing else, it should help you not to take things so personally.

Unfortunately, single-parent households do not have two parents to tag team. I would have loved to have his dad around to take some of the burdens off of my shoulders. It would have been nice for him to shoulder some of the responsibility or at least be there to take over when my strength to fight was utterly gone.

When you are forced to face awful adolescence without the help of the father, it can take a toll on you that wears you down and makes you feel out of control. Believe me. I know how you feel right now!

~Why do things feel different~

The reason things feel different between parent and child during adolescence is that they are. Your child is changing physically, mentally, and emotionally. During this transition, your teen is learning how to be independent, and that means beginning to distance themselves from you, even though they likely do not even realize the reason.

Although this is a natural process, it feels anything but natural when you are going through it. When you can barely get your teen to speak two words to you, it hurts, and it cuts deep into your heart. I can't even begin to count the times I cried into my pillow at night, wishing so badly that things would just go back to normal. Why couldn't my son go back to being the sweet little boy I knew and loved?

Although things never went back to the way they were before my son began to become a man, they did get better, and eventually, they became great. He and I now have a beautiful relationship, and I treasure it. I promise you this too shall pass, and one day, things will get better, mom! You just have to keep going and never give up!

~They prefer friends over mom~

If it hasn't happened already, you may find your teen suddenly wants to be around friends more than they do you. You might even find they are embarrassed to be seen with you.

My son suddenly started wanting me to drop him off a block from the school so his friends wouldn't see him being driven by mom. Please know this is entirely normal and does not have any reflection on you. Even if you were a supermodel, you are still your kid's mom, and therefore, you are completely uncool and embarrassing to be around.

Do not ever attempt to make your teen choose between you and friends. Doing this will only backfire and end up causing a ton of problems you do not want to face. Your teen likely already sees you as the "bad guy" so don't make it worse by making demands that will only drive them further away from you.

~How to cope~

Coping with your teen's emotional mood swings is not easy. You may feel like you are losing your mind in the process. I know I did! The thing to remember is just because your teen is on an emotional roller coaster does not mean you have to get onboard and ride with them. In fact, the best thing you can do when your teen is having an emotional outburst is to ignore it altogether. Believe me, I know that is much easier said than done!

Just remember: your teen needs to reach emotional maturity to become an adult. Emotional maturity is not something we are born with; it comes with time. Try to remember hormonal changes cause the emotional changes your teen is going through. Yes, it all boils down to that one thing, and it's a doozy!

One of the toughest things to do is to keep your composure when you are dealing with an overly emotional teen. Everything is dramatic, and everything that happens to them is either the highlight of their life or the end of the world. It seems there is no in-between.

During those emotionally vulnerable times, it is best to try and be a good listener instead of contending with them. Just listening to them discuss their feelings, without casting any judgment, can relieve some of the pent-up emotions they are feeling.

Whatever you do, do not make light of how they are feeling. Even if you think it is utterly absurd they got so upset because their favorite shirt has a hole in it, make sure to acknowledge and try to understand their feelings.

~Be a good role model~

Believe it or not, your teen is watching what you do and say every day. Do you find yourself being overly emotional at times? Of course, you do; we all do! The thing is, we need to make sure we are a good role model for our kids at all times.

Try to make sure you are healthily handling your emotions. If you are exhibiting emotional outbursts, your teen is likely going to be more prone to having them too.

When you are wrong, make sure you admit it. If your teen sees you making mistakes, apologizing, and learning from them, this will help them to do the same. Always, always, always remember, your teen is going to pay way more attention to what you do rather than what you say.

With all of the bad influences your child will encounter in adolescence; they need to find a good one in you. The following steps will help you to be a better role model for your teen so they will work towards some of the same goals.

- Have your own goals and work towards them. Whether it be education, self-improvement, or conquering fears, make a list of goals and work to achieve each of them.
- Be an honest and humble individual in life, and your teen will have someone to look up to who will provide them with an accurate love-in-action role model.

- Make sure you admit when you are wrong or when you do not have the answer. Your teen needs to know you are far from perfect and regularly make mistakes.
- Be compassionate and forgiving towards everyone, even those who do not deserve it. Yes, this includes your kid's dad!
- Never give up when times get tough so that you can teach your child perseverance.
- Get involved in your community by volunteering or working to make a difference somehow.
- Make sure you exhibit a strong work ethic to teach your teen the importance of earning their way in life, no matter what career choice they make.

Your relationship with your teen may never be what it was before they went through adolescence and this may cause a bit of mourning on your part as a single mom.

It's okay for you to miss what used to be between you and your teen but don't let that cloud over what your new relationship will evolve into. Believe me, my relationship with my son drastically changed through the years but it always seemed to get better, no matter what.

Chapter Five
My Teen's Dad Isn't Around

I believe one of the hardest things about being a single mom is dealing with the father. Some single moms are blessed with having a good relationship with their ex, and I must admit, I envy them.

If your teen's dad isn't in the picture, for whatever reason, it can cause a lot of hurt for both you and your child. Unfortunately, it is the children that suffer the most. How any man or woman could intentionally stay out of their kid's life just astounds me!

It was difficult enough dealing with the questions my son had when he was younger. I regularly heard the following:

"Where is my daddy?"
"Why don't I have a daddy?"
"Does my daddy love me?"
"Why doesn't my daddy live here?"

Sometimes, the questions would just ring out in haunting wave after wave, and I would do my best to stuff down the emotions I was feeling and try to answer my boy's questions without lying, but also without causing him further pain than he was already feeling. It was tough!

As my son grew into adolescence, his anger towards his dad was a significant factor. He had no man around to show him things a dad typically teaches his son. I was there to teach him how to mow the lawn. I taught him how to shave. I taught him how to tie a tie. It was all me.

When my son would spend time with his friends and see how their fathers were so into their lives, it brought out tremendous bitterness in him. I could see him dying inside just a little bit at a time.

~How to help your teen understand~

Frank conversations may not be the most prudent choice when your child is young, but they are often welcome as a kid grows older. It can get a bit tricky when approaching a frank conversation. I did not want to paint his father in a horrible light, but I also knew my son had the right to know the truth.

I knew my son was somewhat bitter towards me. He felt I might be partially to blame for his dad leaving us behind when my son was only a baby. I could envision my son thinking if only mom had been a little sweeter, kept a cleaner house, or been a little prettier; dad might have stayed.

My dilemma was how do I inform my son of the truth without telling him his dad was a no-good, womanizing cheater. I didn't want him going through life blaming me, but I also did not wish to have him hate his father, in the hopes one day, the man might wise up and want to be in his kid's life.

The most important thing I had to convey to my son was that it was in no way his fault. He was a baby, and any father should have been so proud to have him as a son. I had to try and help him see his father just was not ready to be the dad my son needed.

I'm not going to lie. During those moments, I could have honestly punched my ex in the face for putting me in this position. Seeing the tears of bitter anger and hurt flow down my son's face made me livid but I kept those emotions in.

I choked them down because I had to. I, just like my son, hoped one day his father would be a part of his life. If I had planted too much negativity in his young mind, that would never happen.

~Male role models are essential~

No matter the gender of your teen, having a positive male role model is essential. Whether it be an uncle, a grandpa, a friend, a coach, or a pastor, the right male role model is vital for helping a child form sound relationships that will guide them and influence them.

Most single mothers realize their sons need a positive male role model but fail to recognize the need is as strong for their daughters. Kids need to know not all men are like their father. There are good men out there, and they need to be celebrated in your child's life, no matter who they are.

Boys need a male role model to learn how to be – well boys. Even though you can easily teach your teen most of what his dad would, your boy still needs that manly figure to model himself after and to learn how to be a man.

Girls need a strong male role model who will show them trustworthy and honorable men stay and take care of the women in their life. Girls who grow up without a dad often have a difficult time trusting a boyfriend or husband because they always have that fear in the back of their mind that he will eventually leave just like her dad did.

If you are having trouble finding a stable male role model who is willing to be in your child's life consistently, some organizations can help.

- The Boys and Girls Club of America

- Big Brothers Big Sisters

Talking with your church pastor or a counselor can also provide you with information so you can get your teen involved in the right mentorship program. Organizations like The Boys and Girls Club of America can do wonders for a teen who is trying to find their way while living in a single parent household.

My son's male father-figure/role model was his coach. Coach "Bear" as we lovingly called him, was there for my son throughout high school and even beyond. When my son needed a man to talk to, he could always rely on Coach Bear to be there.

~Don't try to be everything for your child~

I think one of the biggest mistakes we single moms make when it comes to overcoming the lack of a father in our kid's life is believing we are all our child needs.

From the beginning, we are forced to do it all, and we can sometimes take on the false mentality that our child doesn't need anyone else in their life because they have a "supermom."

No matter how hard you try, you cannot be everything and everyone your child needs. Today's parent often works overly hard to be there to provide everything they think their kid needs.

Your child needs to look up to more role models than you. I know that might sting just a bit for some single moms out there, but you cannot be a female and try to be a male role model too. The genders are different for a reason, and your child needs to have positive relationships with adults of both sexes so they will be well-rounded.

~What happens if dad suddenly wants a relationship?~

You may not even be able to comprehend the fact your ex might one day show up in your kid's life and suddenly want to be a daddy, but it could happen. I want to help prepare you now so when and if it does occur, you will be ready.

First and foremost, this moment is not about you and what you want. If you are like me, you would prefer to punch your ex in the face and never have to see him again.

This situation is not about you; it's about what your child needs. A child needs their father and having him in their life will help, as long as the father is genuinely committed to being there.

My dad came back one time after leaving my mom. It still haunts me to this day how happy I was one moment and how devastated the next.

I remember my mom made a special dinner and lit candles. My brother and I were so excited he was coming back home, we could barely contain our exuberance. We danced around and shouted with joy the whole night, waiting in expectation.

My dad did come home that night. He brought his belongings and gifts for my brother and me. He ate dinner with us, and we enjoyed the apple pie my mom had lovingly made for the occasion.

The next morning, dad informed us he had made a mistake and shouldn't have come back. My brother screamed and cried, and my dad had to physically remove my brother's clutched fingers from around his legs so he could walk out the door once again.

I have been on both sides of the fence, so I think I have a unique perspective. I know the agony it feels to be that kid who just wants her daddy to love her and I know how it feels to hate my ex for what he is doing to my kid.

~It's all about what's best for your teen~

As long as your teen's father is not involved in any illegal activity and is not a threat to you or your child, you need to leave the decision to your teen. This is one of those moments where being a single mother is even harder than you can imagine because you must relinquish control

Your teen is old enough to be given the facts and to decide on their own. No matter how you feel about the situation, you need to respect your child's feelings, needs, and wants in the matter. If your child does not want any part of his father, then they should not be forced to have a relationship with the man who is a stranger to them.

On the other hand, if your teen decides he wants his dad in his life, it is essential to lay down boundaries and help the process proceed as slowly and smoothly as possible.

The reunion process does not have to happen all at once and probably shouldn't because it can be overwhelming to a child. You need to know your ex is thoroughly committed to being there before he becomes embedded in your child's heart.

I know how it feels to have your dad walk away, come back, and walk away again. It was as if he tore open every wound he had left me with and poured acid in each one.

To this day, I have a very tough time trusting men. Maybe that played a role in the relationship with my ex not working out. When all you know is distrust, it is hard to learn to trust.

~Encourage your child to do what they feel is right~

Make sure to give your teen plenty of space to make their decision. Do not allow their father to contact them in any way until the child is ready. Pushing the relationship too soon could cause a great deal of stress and confusion which can be extremely difficult to deal with when you are already dealing with a hormone-release nightmare as a teen.

In the end, just be there for your kid. You know your child better than their dad ever will. If there is an interest in seeking a relationship, make sure you encourage it and are decisive in dealing with questions and comments.

Your child may remember your ex in a much different light than you do so do not destroy that for them. Instead, just be there to help them in whatever decision they make. Be their most significant support during this time, and you will be much appreciated by your teen who needs your guidance and direction.

Chapter Six
How Do I Foster a Good Relationship with My Teen?

When your teen starts changing during adolescence, it can suddenly seem like your relationship as parent and child is going south. It can honestly feel like a daily battle dealing with a teen's ever-changing emotions.

As a single mom, you likely want your relationship with your child to remain as it always has been. As you see changes happening to your teen, you will soon realize changes must also occur in your relationship.

A lot of we moms mourn the fact our little one isn't so little anymore and may not need us as much as they once did. Although this is what is supposed to happen naturally, it can still be hard for a single mother. I know it was tough for me!

The most challenging part of being the mom of a teen, especially a single one, is letting go. Knowing when to let go is essential for helping your teen mature into a self-reliant adult that can make sound decisions. From one mom to another, knowing this is what is supposed to happen does not make it any easier to face.

~Don't relinquish your role as parent~

One of the biggest mistakes a single mom can make with her teen is trying to be their friend instead of their parent. While there is nothing wrong with being a friend and confidante to your child, that friendship needs to remain within the boundaries of parenthood.

You cannot suddenly become a peer to your teen. They need you, mom, in that position you have always held. This is not the time to switch up roles and suddenly become the "hang out" buddy with your teen. If you end up doing this, you will go over the line you once drew in the sand with your child, and it is challenging to go back and gain control after that happens.

Remember, mom, you have the life experience and understanding your child's friends do not. Your teen needs your guidance as a parent and role model, not as one of the guys or gals they hang with on a regular basis.

Your teen is going to need to start branching out on their own, but they need you
there as a safety net they can fall back on when they inevitably fail. Your teen is going to have a love/hate relationship with the boundaries you put in place, so be ready for that.

On the one hand, no teen wants to be told what they can and cannot do; after all, they know everything remember? (Big eye roll here!) On the other hand, your teen secretly respects you for putting boundaries in place and even appreciates them. You will likely never hear them say that, but they do.

~Three crucial elements of a stable parent and child relationship~

Three essential values are a part of any relationship but are especially vital for the relationship between a parent and a child. If any of these values are missing, the parent and child relationship is based on a shaky foundation that could crumble at any moment.

1. **Trust** is one of the principal elements of a parent and child relationship. Not only must you be able to trust your teen, but they must also be able to trust you. Remember, your teen is just like any other human being, you must earn their trust; it is not merely given.
2. **Security** is another significant component of having a healthy relationship with your teen. This is where boundaries become vital. Offering protection in a relationship is also all about acceptance and letting your child know they are unconditionally loved, and you are always there for them.
3. **Love** is one of the fundamental constituents of your parent and child relationship. Telling your teen how much you love them is a good start, but your actions will convey your love much more effectively than words ever could. Never forget the power of a big mama bear hug or saying a simple, "I'm so proud of you!"

If any of these elements is lacking in your relationship with your teen, it is not going to be easy, but you can still begin to rebuild slowly. I know the love is there! Otherwise, you would not be worried enough about your relationship with your teen to be reading this book.

~Ways to develop a closer relationship with your teen~

This might sound old-fashioned to today's generation but eating around the family dinner table is tremendously essential. Today's parents are busier than ever and so are their kids so this pastime is becoming a faint memory.

Study after study has been carried out over the years on the importance of family dinners around the table. It is a small thing you can start doing with your teen at least a couple of nights a week.

Make sure the television and phones are shut off, and it's just you and your kid, talking, laughing, and enjoying one another's company. You will be amazed at the difference this can make in your teen and even in yourself.

One study carried out on 5,000 teens in Minnesota revealed regular dinners around the family table significantly reduced depression and suicidal thoughts in the teens. Other studies have found correlations between family dinners and reduced promiscuity, drug and alcohol use, and school problems.

It might seem like such an insignificant measure to take but eating dinner at home with your teen offers an excellent opportunity for communication. Everyone likes to eat, and while your teen is eating, they are more likely to engage in open and honest discussions with you.

Asking them how their day went can open up an entire dialogue of discussion, as long as you are willing to sit back and listen. Ever wonder why your teen is always talking to their friends more than you?

Your teen's friends listen without judgment. It is the key to successfully opening the doors to a better relationship between parent and child. If you find it difficult to get your kid talking, make some dinner and set the table and I bet you will see changes!

Chapter Seven
I'm Worried About My Teen's Friends

When I was growing up, things were so much different than they are now. There was no Internet (yes, I am that old!) and the world seemed to be a much less frightening place than it is now.

My mom knew all of my friends because they were either over at my house or she was driving me to theirs on a regular basis. Our moms were friends too so there were no secret friendships.

Today, our kids have what seems to be a significant advantage over our generation, but I wonder if that is the case. With the Internet and cell phones, teens today have the world at their fingertips, and this can be scary for single moms!

We have all read the horror stories about kids making friendships online and really bad things happening as a result. Although we want our teens to have a certain level of freedom, giving them too much can be dangerous. Keeping track of your teen's friends is indeed a challenge, but it is not impossible if you follow the strategies in this chapter.

~Keeping your teen cyber safe~

Having the world at their fingertips is excellent for learning and exploration but can also be a parent's worst nightmare. If your teen is consistently on their cell phone or the computer, you likely have concerns over what they are doing and who they are communicating with.

With cell phones in their hands, teens can get into a world of trouble, including unknowingly forming relationships with child predators. There is also the threat of cyberbullying to worry about.

Although you cannot be with your teen every single time they access their cell phone or the computer, you can put safeguards in place to make sure your teen is limited on what apps they can download and how long they can use the Internet.

There are even "spy apps" that allow you to record images and keystrokes that are made on their cellphone or computer keyboard. From one single mom to another, I think it's best if we attempt to trust our teens first before we employ such drastic measures as spying.

Prevention is the key, and this means talking to your kid about the dangers in such a way that will make them fully understand what can happen if they are not wise in the cyber world.

Teens need to know once they put something out in cyberspace, be it a photo or a comment, it can easily be shared with other people and could potentially ruin a teen's life. Unfortunately, most teens feel "invincible" and think it will never happen to them.

As a single mom, you have the right to know all the passwords for all of your teen's social media and email accounts. Let them know you will not always log in to check behind them but make them understand you do reserve the right to use that power.

It's the same as you being able to log into the Internet at work. Your boss has likely set up a privacy statement that lets you know they could view your accounts and information at any time.

The big message to get across to your teen: "If you wouldn't say it or show it at the dinner table with me, then don't say it or post it online!"

~My teen's friends are a terrible influence~

Almost every mom on the planet has faced this issue and been worried about their teen. When our kids meet a new friend, we can often surmise right away the other kid is not a good fit.

I found myself in quite a dilemma when my son became friends with a kid I knew was no good for him. This kid was rude, and I suspected he was teaching my son things I did not want him to know at such a young age.

The problem was, I immediately started hounding my son about this kid. I let him know I did not like the boy and pushed him towards ending the friendship. Guess what happened? Instead of my son doing as I requested, he became angry and stood up for his friend.

I just didn't understand, he would say. He thought I didn't know what I was talking about. My anger over this friend I thought was a lousy choice ended up pushing my son closer to the wrong decision instead of farther away.

Its obvious teens do not want their parents meddling in their friendships but what is a single mom to do when she is apprehensive about her kid's friends, and for a good reason? I learned the hard way, and my approach backfired, so I am here to help you avoid making the same mistake. I like to call this my stealth approach, and I have shared it with many struggling single moms and two-parent families. It works!

1. One of the worst things you can do is to say, "I don't like your friend!" To a teen, this is not a good reason and will likely make them defensive, just like my son was. Instead, take a more practical approach. Let your teen know their

friend is developing a bad reputation and if they hang out with that person, the rep will become theirs. Let them know this could affect their ability to make other friends and even prevent them from meeting that special someone.
2. Make your home a haven for your teen's friends to hang out. Allow your teen to invite their friend over often. If your teen's friend is bad news, they are not going to want to hang around under your nose all the time and will eventually drop your teen for another friend whose parents let them do what they want.
3. Set appropriate boundaries. Your teen needs to learn how to make friends and what to look for in a friend. This means allowing them sometimes to make mistakes and learn from them. Setting boundaries means you are allowing your teen to be friends with this person as long as your child remembers the rules of the household and how they are to behave themselves in and away from your presence.
4. If your teen still keeps hanging out with this person you do not like, sit down and have a discussion. Ask your child why they like this friend. Share with your child the valid reasons why you are concerned about the friend. In the

end, mom, you are going to have to let go and hope and pray your teen figures out this "friend" is not a good friend to have. It might take time, but you need to trust your teen to do the right thing and choose wisely. It may take some negative repercussions happening first.

Let's face it; you are not going to like all of your teen's friends. We must realize all families are different and many kids are practically raising themselves. Try giving the friend a chance and take time to get to know them.

I have misjudged some of my son's friends solely by their appearance or how I perceived them. Believe it or not, I was sometimes wrong in my judgment and ended up liking my son's friends once I got to know them. Maybe you will too.

If the friend is indeed a bad apple, your teen will eventually realize it and lose interest. Unless your teen is putting themselves in actual danger with this friend, try to let it go and wait and see what happens. Your teen might just actually surprise you in the way they deal with things!

~How to help your teen choose the right friends~

We all worry about the harmful effects of our teens making poor friendship choices. After all, your teen's peers often have much more of an influence over the decisions they make than you do.

Study after study has been published showing the importance of friendship at every age. Having a close friend gives teens higher levels of self-esteem and promotes their overall feelings of wellbeing. How can you help guide your teen towards making the right friends without making it seem as if you are lording over them?

When your child was younger, it was indeed comfortable for you to be able to control their friendships. You could set up play dates and organize activities that would draw your child towards the right friendship choices.

When your child gets into the teen years, orchestrating their friendships is no longer as easy as it once was. Whether your teen is having difficulty making friends or choosing the right ones, this section is helpful.

Making friends is a skill that can be taught and the earlier you teach it to your child, the better equipped they will be to make sound friendship choices in their teens and later in life.

Learning how to make friends involves a great deal of self-awareness and practice. You can help your child reflect on different aspects of themselves, and this will help them to choose friends that build them up instead of tearing them down.

~Help your teen reflect on what makes them a good friend~

For your teen to make good friends, they need to *be* a good friend. It's not enough to only seek out someone that has the same interests. Ask your teen, "What qualities do you have that would make someone want to reach out to you and be your friend?" Your teen needs to think about this question and figure out if they are offering attributes that would make others want to be their friend.

The art of conversation is critical for making friends but today's kids often lack these skills because they communicate more behind a screen than they do face-to-face. Practicing small talk with your teen will help them to learn how to keep the conversation naturally flowing and help them to learn to listen more than they talk.

One of the most challenging things teens deal with when they are having trouble making friends is latching on too tightly to the first person who shows them any attention. They end up pushing too hard to make the friendship a close one and ultimately push the potential friend away.

It happens to us adults as well. Teach your teen that not everyone is going to be their best friend. Help them learn to take things slowly and let the friendship naturally develop into what it is meant to be, whether it be a BFF or merely a friend they eat lunch with and talk to in class.

~Do your best to guide them – The rest is up to them~

In the end, you are not going to be able to hold your teen's hand and help them make the right friendship choices. Growing into a stable adult will mean they need to make mistakes and learn from them. The only way they can do this is by you letting them go as much as possible, while also keeping a watchful eye and making sure they are not in danger.

Don't try to micromanage your teen's relationships or it will certainly backfire on you. Instead, guide them and instruct them and then leave it up to them to make the decisions. If a friendship turns sour, never say, "I told you so!" even if you knew from the beginning it would.

Chapter Eight
My Teen Is Not Responsible

Teaching a teen to be responsible is a tremendous undertaking, especially when a single parent did not start early in the younger years. Teens tend to act as if they are in their own little world and nothing they do or do not do affects anyone else. It is our job as a parent to teach them otherwise, and boy is it tough!

Responsibility is one of the areas I struggled a lot with while teaching my son as a single mom. As he grew older, I needed to be able to rely on him to help me, but it seemed he was not yet prepared. Just to share how frustrating it can be teaching a teen to be responsible, let me share this little story.

I was working a job that I liked and had finally been given the opportunity to obtain a higher position in the company. My boss wanted to talk things over so; I invited her over to dinner without thinking it through first.

I had made a list of chores for my son to do while I was at work so the house would be sparkling when I got home. He was out of school for the summer, and I thought he could surely help me with all the free time he had on his hands.

    Before I left for work that morning, I went over the list with him as he gobbled down a bowl of cereal and barely took off his headphones to hear me. He assured me he knew what to do and rolled his eyes as if I was overly dramatic.

    Again, I made sure he understood how much this night meant to me, to both of us. He promised to do the work so I could finish dinner when I got home.

    To be sure the work would be done as promised, I even called him a couple of times to check in, and he assured me he was on top of things. Nothing was done when I got home. To my dismay, my son had never even picked up the list from the table where I had left it.

    I exploded! I was livid and likely said many things I shouldn't have. He became angry and didn't seem to "get" why I was so freaked out. It was at that moment that I felt like going in my room, shutting the door, and giving up. But, I couldn't do that! I was the responsible adult, and I had to show my son how to be accountable too.

We rushed around, and I made my son do all the chores he had promised to do. The night ended up going well, and my boss would have never guessed the chaos that had occurred just before her arrival.

Thankfully, I got the job promotion, and my son and I both learned a valuable lesson that night. I learned he was not ready to be fully trusted to be responsible and he learned if I gave him something to do and he didn't do it, significant problems could erupt!

Looking back, it almost seems comical now, and I can even smile about his irresponsibility, but it certainly wasn't funny then. Let me tell you what I did to help my son become responsible without pulling out every last hair I had on my head.

~The art of getting your teen to do chores~

Notice how I titled this little section? It indeed is an art form getting a teen to do anything, especially chores. We think as single moms, the least our kid can do is to do a few chores now and again to help us out, right?

The problem is, getting the teen to do the chores can become a full-time job. Half the time, they don't do them at all, and when you do get them to do their duties, they often give you the lovely eye roll or the angry look. This is a time when your patience is going to be truly tested while being a single mother.

When dealing with getting your teen to do their chores, you are likely thinking, "If only they would just do what I tell them to" and your kid is likely thinking, "If they would just leave me alone!" So, is it possible for you and your teen to get on the same page and work together to get those necessary chores done without World War III happening every single time?

~Your teen needs to be responsible for their messes~

I think most parents can agree; a teen needs to be responsible for cleaning up their messes. A parent should never clean their teen's room. If you are cleaning your teen's room, make sure you stop right now. Your teen needs to learn the messes they make are their responsibility.

As a part of teaching them responsibility, it is essential to show them how to wash their own clothes properly. If they refuse, they will be the ones embarrassed because they have to wear yesterday's stained T-shirt to school.

No matter how much your teen protests or tries to make you feel guilty, do not cave in and do their laundry for them. Mom, they are old enough to do this little chore for themselves, and it will teach them to be responsible for making sure their clothes are clean and ready for school or outings with friends.

You have got to do your part and stop doing everything for your teen. If you bail them out each time they "forget" to wash their clothes, they will continue to forget. Instead of getting fed up with them and figuring it is easier to do it yourself, call them out on their mess and make them address it.

If you don't wash their clothes and they don't either, they are going to find themselves being forced to wear dirty clothes. If they leave their clothes around, ask them is this a donate pile.

This statement should clue them in and have them pick up the clothes and take them to their room. If they continue to leave the pile there, perhaps you will need to take more drastic actions and donate the items.

Now if you are a gentle mom like I once was, you will think the above statement is way too harsh. Once you have been through years of yelling and pleading with your teen to pick up their clothes off the floor, you might just change your mind!

~Paid and unpaid chores should be introduced~

Your teen will need to be aware of the everyday chores that are expected of them. These chores are not paid duties. Your teen needs to know they are a part of something bigger than themselves, which is your single-parent home. If you pay your teen to do something they should be doing freely, this is not helping them to grow in maturity or become responsible.

Things, like cleaning their room, taking out the trash, and loading the dishwasher should be considered everyday, non-pay chores. If you want to avoid the "I didn't know" excuse your teen is likely to throw at you, post a list, so it is blatantly clear.

While you do not want to nag, you do need to make your teen aware of their responsibility and the repercussions of not doing their chores. Never, ever, ever offer money or bribery for doing everyday chores; it will certainly backfire on you.

~Introducing paid chores~

Okay, this is where the lessons in responsibility can get a little interesting for you as a single mom and for your teen. Teaching your teen it is advantageous to go above and beyond the call of duty, sometimes has to involve a little monetary encouragement.

Being a single mom means often having to hire people to do certain chores for you, such as washing your car, mowing the grass, or cleaning out the gutters. These jobs should be introduced to your teen as a means for them to make side money. Teach them the importance of earning their money, and they will likely learn to be much more responsible in their spending.

Let your teen know; these jobs are considered different from the day-to-day chores they usually do. Your teen needs to know they are replacing a professional and will be held to the same standards which means they must fully complete the job and do it correctly if they want to be paid.

Next time your teen comes around asking for money for movie tickets or that new video game, point them to the job board you have created and let them start earning that spending money by helping you out around the house. They may grumble and complain, as they always do, but you might be surprised to see them pull out that old bucket and soap to start washing your car.

Chapter Nine
My Teen Is Not Doing Well in School

Your teen likely is either indifferent to school or hates it; there is rarely any in-between when it comes to teens. If you are lucky enough to have a teen that loves school and is getting good grades, then you may not even need to read this chapter.

Unfortunately, the majority of single mothers deal with some degree of issues with their teen and school so this chapter is devoted to helping solo parents encourage their child to do the best they can at school, with as few hiccups along the way as possible.

My son loved elementary school, but when middle school and later high school came around, he quickly formed a hate relationship with his education. His once stellar record of being on the honor roll and having perfect attendance began to take a downward spiral, adding another worry to my rapidly growing list I consulted every day, primarily when trying to go to sleep at night.

Before we launch into this subject, I want us to think about something that is important in gauging how we respond to our teen who is struggling in school. Teens today are under so much more academic pressures than we were in school. The weight of standardized tests and the considerable peer pressure and bullying many teens face can make them hate school, and if we think about things from their point of view, we might be able to understand their ambivalence towards their education experience better.

~How to help teens who are being bullied~

As a single mother, it can be heart-wrenching to learn your child is being bullied in school. Unfortunately, many teens do not share this vital information with their parents because they are ashamed.

Each year, many teens end their lives because of bullying, so it is critical single mothers know what to look for, so they will know if their teen is being bullied at school, on the bus, or even online. The following are some of the most common signs a teen will exhibit when they are being bullied.

- Declining grades or a loss of interest in school (this also occurs for other reasons)
- Unexplained injuries

- Frequent bouts of headaches and stomach aches
- Changes in eating habits
- Comes home with missing or destroyed belongings
- Sudden and severe decreases in self-esteem
- Avoiding social situations
- Self-destructive behaviors

It is important to stay engaged in conversations about bullying with your teen. Your teen needs to know they can come to you and get help, no matter what is going on in their life.

If your teen comes to you and tells you they are being bullied, it is essential you remain calm and do not overreact. It is imperative you show your child unconditional love and give them praise for having the guts to come and voluntarily tell you what is going on at school.

While it is critical you do not overreact; it is just as important you do not under-react. Your teen needs to know you understand the full implications of bullying and how it is negatively affecting them. If you brush it under the rug, your teen will likely never come to you again for help.

As a single mother, it is your responsibility to make sure your child is safe and if this means getting the school officials involved, so be it. Be there to encourage your child and get them the help they need.

~What to do when your teen is getting bad grades~

Many parents deal with their teen getting poor grades and this is not merely a single mom issue. As a mom, single or not, you want your teen to do well in school so they can go on to college and have a bright future.

If your teen is doing poorly in school, it is crucial you find out why. Many factors can come into play when a kid is suddenly bringing home unexpected bad grades.

Outside of bullying and emotional/mental health concerns, most teens either have poor grades because they cannot perform at a higher level or because they are underachieving.

Testing is a proven method of ensuring your teen is performing at grade level. If your teen is not getting the good grades they once were, it is wise for you to reach out to their teacher and review test scores. Specialized testing may need to be conducted to ensure there are no learning barriers that are preventing the better grades.

When a teen is getting poor grades due to a lack of ability, they should never be made to feel bad or punished in any way. Instead, these teens need encouragement and extra help, even if it means hiring a tutor.

~Some teens just do not care~

If your teen just does not care about school but has the potential to get much better grades, this section will help. A lot of teens, my son included, merely have a problem staying on task and managing their time.

Friends and fun are always more important than homework and grades. When your teen is not doing as well as they should be in school, it is time to enact a punishment/reward system that is fair and will help encourage success.

No, this does not mean you go to the extreme and expect straight A's. Such a high expectation may not be warranted or even healthy for your teen. Instead, expect them to do their very best and set reasonable rules with your teen.

1. Decide which grades are unacceptable and the consequences of getting these grades.
2. Decide which grades are acceptable. Acceptable grades have neither a consequence or a reward.
3. Exceptional grades mean your teen is going above and beyond in their pursuit of education, and they should be rewarded accordingly.

Your teen's education is vital for their future, but it can be highly stressful feeling like you are continually having to push your teen towards getting their homework done or studying for tests.

As a single mother, you need to stay in contact with your teen's school and teachers on a regular basis. Staying in touch and checking your teen's progress will help you to determine problem areas before your teen entirely slips from their expected goals.

I know it's not easy keeping your teen on track, and they may not always get the grades you would love to show off to others, but the important thing is your teen needs to be trying their best and making steady progress towards their educational goals. Even though it is harder to push them towards success when you are doing it alone, you can do it because you are fully equipped to help your teen succeed!

Chapter Ten
Encouragement for Single Mothers

In this book, you and I have talked a lot about many of the issues you face in raising your teen as a single mom. With much of the book focused on your teen, now it is time for us to focus on you.

I would be remiss if I left you without being encouraged. This entire book is devoted to helping single moms feel empowered to raise their teens alone, even when they feel exhausted, also when they think they do not have the ability. I want you to finish reading this book and feel like the superwoman you are!

Being a single mother, as I have said many times, is one of the toughest jobs imaginable. All too often, we are ostracized in society and made to feel guilty because we do not fit the norms of what is expected in a familial unit.

No, this was likely not the life you envisioned for yourself and your child. Most of us grow up with the fantasy of believing in the white knight or at least the white picket fence.

No matter how off course your life is from what you had hoped it to be, this does not mean you have failed. Others may have failed you, situations may have been harsh, but you are a fighter and not a quitter.

If you were a quitter, you wouldn't have picked up this book and started reading. If you were a quitter, you would have done it long ago! The fact is, you are a survivor and you can and will raise your teen and survive doing it.

~Hold your head high, single mom~

I don't care how many times this life has knocked you down. It doesn't matter how many times you have cried yourself to sleep or felt like you were impossibly inadequate. You are more than enough, and your role as a single mom should be celebrated and honored.

If you feel like a second-class citizen because you are a solo parent, I want you to stop that stinking thinking right now. Not all moms stay and fight. Not all moms have made it as far as you have.

Even if you have scraped knees and runny mascara, you are still in control and will fight for your child with your last breath. Each time you want to give up and think you can't do it, I want you to remember you are a fighter and you can and will succeed as a single mom.

Things may not be roses and rainbows but each day you get through will give you more strength to make it through the next. Before long, you and your teen will not only be surviving together but thriving.

~Start a single mom journal~

I've tried to share some bits and pieces of my journey as a single mom who made it through and raised my son, who is now a young adult. No, I do not consider myself a perfect mom and my son doesn't either. We often laugh at how genuinely imperfect I was and am, and I believe that is healthy for us both.

One of the things that helped me in my journey of being a solo parent was journaling. I want to take you back to those many years ago when you kept a diary and wrote down your most personal thoughts and feelings.

Let's go back to that! Let's embrace our ability to write down what hurts us, what makes us smile, and how we managed each day. I want you to do this on both good and bad days. There are two reasons for journaling, and both will help you immensely.

Number one – Journaling will help you to get those feelings out, so they do not become bottled up inside. It is one of the healthiest ways of dealing with negative emotions, and you will be amazed at how much better it makes you feel.

Number two – Journaling will help you to be able to look back on the darker days and see how far you have come in your parent and child relationship. This will give you a real insight into your progression as a single mother and encourage you to keep going, even when the days seem darker and more difficult than ever before.

~Stop feeling guilty about every single thing~

Every mom I have ever talked to, even if they are not single, has unimaginable guilt. A lot of the blame we deal with is internal, but some of it comes from society, our families, and even our own kids.

Guilt can eat you alive if you allow it. I want you to be free of your guilt once and for all. I want you to know you have done your very best and that is what truly matters as a single mom. As moms, we can feel guilty about so many things, to the point it becomes almost ridiculous.

- We feel guilty if we are too strict and then turn around and feel guilty if we are not rigid enough.
- We feel guilty if we spend time out having fun and then feel guilty if we don't feel guilty while we are out having fun.

You see, there is always something we as single moms are going to worry about or feel guilty over. Some of the guilt trips we put ourselves on are asinine.

As a single mother, there are five things you can do right now to start overcoming the guilt you feel and embracing your imperfections and seeing them as just perfect.

1. You must realize you are going to have to let some things go and you cannot control everything.
2. You are in a competition with no other parent.
3. Start looking at the future and the big picture it represents instead of the day-to-day mistakes.
4. Live in the moment and learn to enjoy it.
5. Laugh a lot, especially at yourself.

~You are a treasure, single mom~

You may not feel like it, but I want you to know you are a treasure! You could have been irresponsible and walked away just like your teen's father did, but you chose to rise above your discomfort and refused to take the easy way out.

I applaud you, single mom! I know it hasn't been easy and sometimes you feel like you just want to get off this roller coaster of life, but I encourage you to keep going and keep searching for those brighter days, even if you only see a glimpse of them here and there.

One day, you will be able to look back on your journey and realize you did it! You may not have done it like other mothers or even as you planned to, but you did it.

I hope by reading this book, you have found your inner courage to push through the obstacles and problems that stand in the way of you living a fulfilling life as a single mom. I hope, through my struggles, you will be able to stand tall and with confidence when you face the same.

No, the life of a single mom is not easy, but it is worth it. When you realize your child is grown and you made it, you will be able to look back on these hard days and rejoice because you survived.

I hope that each night your head hits the pillow, you are reminded of some of these words, and they give you the courage to close your eyes, thank God, and rest with hope in your future.

Now, the rest is up to you. I've given you the tools to help you be a success and to help you to know how to deal with some of the most common obstacles that single moms of teens face.

I have faith in you that you can rise above the cards you have been dealt and find inner peace and courage to fight. Now, get out there and live that life you have always dreamed of living, even if it just means you and your teen are challenging the world alone!

Conclusion

No mom is perfect whether she has an army by her side or is doing it all alone. In the hustle and bustle of your everyday flow, I want you to be reminded that you may not be perfect, but each day, you are getting better and better at this thing we call being a single mother.

There are going to be days you can't stop laughing and other days when you can't seem to stop crying. I want you to fully embrace both of these types of days because that is what being a solo parent is all about.

It would take volumes to cover all of the issues a single mom of a teen faces while raising her child but this book has focused on some of the most common you will face.

I hope it helps you to rise above each obstacle and find common ground with your teen so you can not only put up with them but enjoy being around your teen.

When times get hard, pull this book back out and use it as a reference or a source of encouragement. My hope for you is with each new day, you grow just a little bit stronger and can look back and realize you were much more courageous than you ever gave yourself credit for being.

If you know of other struggling single moms, who need direction or just to know someone else feels just like they do, purchase a copy as a gift for them. They will thank you immensely for shedding light on a subject that is often avoided in the mainstreams of society.

Thank you for all you do, mom! If no one else ever thanks you for the hard work you put in each and every day, I want you to know that I do. God bless you as you strive to raise your teen alone! It does get better!

I want to thank you for buying this book. Would you do me a favor? It would help me if you would take a moment and write an honest review. Reviews really help with sales and I would appreciate it very much.

God Bless
Donna Joyce

Made in the USA
Middletown, DE
23 December 2018